WTB_Mark

A Living and Active Stage Adaptation of

Mark's Gospel

by Steve Cook
©2015 Five Talents Audio

WTB_Mark: A Living and Active Stage Adaptation of Mark's Gospel

Published by Five Talents Audio
Copyright 2015 by Five Talents Audio
ISBN13: 978-0-9821616-8-5

Printed in the USA
ALL RIGHTS RESERVED
No part of this publication may be reproduced, stored in a retrieval system or transmitted in any form or by any means - electronic, mechanical, photocopying, recording or otherwise - without prior written permission.

For more information:
Five Talents Audio
770-518-8336

Living and Active

This production relies on a unique form of sound design which helps the actors bring the Word to life in fresh and exciting new ways. It is based on my one-man, Scripture-only audio drama recording called "Witness The Bible: Mark". It includes cinematic music and sound effects throughout (think Jonathan Park), which are meticulously timed out to coincide with the action. **This makes the direction much simpler and offers the actors a wonderful opportunity for long-passage Scripture memorization in a very active and fun setting.** It is prop-less with a very simple set and costumes. No lights are required, although a few simple cues are suggested, if feasible.

The soundtrack directions are very detailed and always appear in **BOLD**. *(e.g. begin **WTB_Mark01u_mix** or **SFX - AMAZED CROWD UNDERNEATH**)*. The soundtrack is lifted directly from my audio recording. To get an idea of what the finished product is supposed to sound like, lo-fi audio samples may be streamed for free at the bottom of the Bible Gateway Devotionals page. Just click on "Mark". The free link to the hi-fi underscores you will need for the production are given at the bottom of the Contents page. A link to purchase the fully mixed hi-fi recording is also there.

Thank you for deciding to present "WTB_Mark". I truly believe both you and your audience will experience Jesus' sanctifying supernatural power at work in this play simply by memorizing it and speaking it back to each other actively in community. But I also believe you'll have a lot of fun doing it, too! Remember, dramatization and storytelling were our ONLY means of passing on God's Word for almost HALF of our recorded existence, until a guy named Moses began to write it all down about 3400 years ago. So God must think there's something to it!

Should you have any questions, please don't hesitate to call 404.579.6864. I am always available to help and pray with you.

Have fun and may God be magnified by your presentation!
Steve

CONTENTS

Act 1 (Galilee and Judea)

Chapter 1   (Mark 1:1-34_40-45_2:1-11)   1
Chapter 2   (Mark 2:12-3:4)   8
Chapter 3   (Mark 3:4-35)   10
Chapter 4   (Mark 4:1-20,26-29,35-41)   14
Chapter 5   (Mark 5:1-17_6:7-13,30)   17
Chapter 6   (Mark 6:31-56)   20
Chapter 7   (Mark 7:1-23)   23
Chapter 8   (Mark 8:22-38_9:1)   26
Chapter 9   (Mark 9:2-13,31-32)   28
Chapter 10 (Mark 10:13-34)   31

Intermission: 10-15 minutes

Act 2 (Jerusalem)

Chapter 11 (Mark 11:1-11,15-18,27-33)   34
Chapter 12 (Mark 12:28-34)   37
Chapter 13 (Mark 13:1-20,24-37)   38
Chapter 14 (All Verses)   42
Chapter 15 (All Verses)   52
Chapter 16 (All Verses)   60

Hi-Fi mp3 underscores are available for FREE at:
www.audioadrenalineinc.com/Audiobooks/WTB/Mark/WTBK/3948576&uRFDc78/WTB_Mark_underscores.zip

Lo-Fi audio sample of "Witness The Bible: Mark" is available for FREE at:
www.biblegateway.com/devotionals/

Hi-Fi audio of "Witness The Bible: Mark" is available for purchase at:
www.witnessthebible.com

Cast

Chorus #1
Chorus #2
Chorus #3
Jesus
Peter
John
James
Magdelene
John Baptist / Bystander #1
Voice of God / Angel at the Tomb
Witness #1 / Pilate
Witness #2 / Centurion
Witness #3 / Matthew
Leper / Blind Man / Bystander #2
Scribe #1 / Elder #1
Scribe #2 / Elder #2
Pharisee / Judas
Disciple / Rich Man
Scribe #3 / Possessed Man / Trial Witness
Maid #1 / Mary, mother of James
Maid #2 / Salome
Simon The Zealot / Worshiper #2
Bartholemew / Worshiper #1
Thomas / Worshiper #3 / Andrew
Thaddaeus / Villager / Philip
Legion / Old Scribe / High Priest

Except for the first eight characters listed, these are only suggestions. Characters may be assigned differently at the director's discretion. Just be careful not to create confusion for the audience.

No one should ever be offstage for long, but seated or standing on 3 risers (or bleachers) upstage when not involved in the action. Actors without speaking parts in scenes should be used as "extras" whenever possible.

WTB_Mark

A Living and Active Stage Adaptation of Mark's Gospel
in Two Acts
by Steve Cook

Act 1

Chapter 1 (Mark 1:1-34_40-45_2:1-11)

*(begin **WTB_Mark01u_mix** on soundtrack)*

Chorus #1: *(offstage mic, dark stage)*
The beginning of the Gospel of Jesus Christ, the Son of God. As it is written in the Prophets, Behold, I send my messenger before your face, who shall prepare your way before you. The voice of him that cries in the wilderness, is: Prepare the way of the Lord. Make His paths straight.

(during the next speech, all enter except the 3 Choruses, as stage becomes dimly lit. John mimes baptizing a few people while the rest take their places on risers US)

(SFX - WATER)

Chorus #2: *(offstage)*
John baptized in the wilderness, and preached the baptism of repentance, for remission of sins. And all the country of Judea, and they of Jerusalem went out to him, and were all baptized by him in the river Jordan, confessing their sins.
Now John was clothed with camel's hair, and wore a belt of a skin around his waist. And he ate locusts and wild honey. And preached, saying,

John Baptist: A Stronger than I comes after me, Whose sandals I am not worthy to stoop down and unloose! Truth it is, I have baptized you with water. But He will baptize you with the holy Ghost!

Chorus #3: *(as he/she and the other two Choruses enter from different locations. Chorus #1 and #2 move to positions DSL and DSR, while Chorus #3 remains upstage of the action, on the first riser)*

And it came to pass in those days, that Jesus came from Nazareth, a city of Galilee, and was baptized by John in Jordan.

(SFX - WATER)

And as soon as He came out of the water, John saw the heavens torn apart,

(SFX – 'HEAVENS TORN APART')

and the holy Ghost descending upon Jesus like a dove.

Then there was a voice from heaven, saying,

God: *(RECORDED)* **YOU ARE MY BELOVED SON, IN WHOM I AM WELL PLEASED.**

(OMINOUS MUSIC)

Chorus #1: *(DSL, spoken while all actors move back to risers and wait)*

And immediately the Spirit drove Him into the wilderness. And He was there in the wilderness forty days, and was tempted by Satan. He was also with the wild beasts. And the Angels ministered to Him.

(SFX – CITY AND MUSIC CHANGE UNDER)

Chorus #2: *(DSR, as Jesus moves down from risers SL and a crowd of 5 or 6 moves down CS)*

And after John was committed to prison, Jesus came into Galilee, preaching the Gospel of the kingdom of God. *(exit SR)*

Jesus: *(to crowd)* The time is fulfilled, and the kingdom of God is at hand! Repent and believe the Gospel!

(crowd disperses back to risers, with Peter, Andrew, James and John remaining behind, "mending their nets" in pairs CS and DSR. Chorus #3 emerges from crowd and moves DSL where Chorus #2 was)

Chorus #3: And as He walked by the sea of Galilee, He saw Simon, and Andrew his brother, casting a net into the sea, for they were fishermen.

Jesus: *(stopping CS)* Follow me. And I will make you fishers of men.

(SFX - OARS BEING LAID DOWN IN BOATS)

Chorus #3: *(as Peter and Andrew rise to follow Jesus DSR to James and John, also miming mending their nets)*

And immediately they left their nets, and followed Him. And when He had gone a little further, He saw James the son of Zebedee, and John his brother, as they were in the ship, mending their nets. And He called them and they left their father Zebedee in the ship with his hired servants, and went after Him.

*(all four follow Jesus OSR, **SFX – ZEBEDEE AND HIS SERVANTS: "JOHN, WHAT ARE YOU DOING!?!...***)*

Chorus #3: *(DSL)* So they entered into Capernaum. And immediately on the Sabbath day Jesus entered into the Synagogue, and taught. And they were astonished at His doctrine. For He taught them as one that had authority, and not as the Scribes.

*(**SFX - DEMONIC TRANSITION AND MUSIC** as demon-possessed man enters SL simultaneously with Jesus and the four others re-entering SR. They meet CS)*

Chorus #3: And there was in their Synagogue a man in whom was an unclean spirit. And he cried out, saying,

Possessed Man: Ah, what have we to do with You, O Jesus of Nazareth?! Are You come to destroy us? I know what You are: even The Holy One of God!!

(a crowd of 5 or 6 steps down from risers and gathers around them)

Jesus: Hold your peace! And come out of him!

*(**SFX – DEMON COMING OUT UNDERNEATH**)*

Chorus #3: And the unclean spirit shook him. And cried with a loud voice. And came out of him.

*(**SFX - AMAZED CROWD UNDERNEATH**)*

And they were all amazed. *(exit SL)*

Witness #1: *(from the crowd)* What thing is this?

Witness #2: *(from the crowd)* And what new doctrine is this?

Witness #3: *(from the crowd)* For He commands even the foul spirits with authority, and they obey him!

(SFX – FADE, CHORAL MUSIC UP AND UNDER. As Jesus and followers exit SL)

Chorus #1: *(DSR)* And immediately his fame spread abroad throughout all the region bordering on Galilee.

(Jesus enters USR with followers and crosses down to Peter's "house" DSL, with a crowd of 5 or 6 lined up outside the "door")

And they entered into the house of Simon and Andrew, with James and John. And Simon's mother-in-law lay sick of a fever. And they told him of Her. And He came and took her by the hand, and lifted her up, and the fever left her. And she ministered to them.

And when evening came, they brought to Him all that were diseased, and them that were possessed with devils. And the whole city was gathered together at the door. And He healed many who were sick of diverse diseases. And He cast out many devils, and commanded the devils not to say that they knew Him.

(person at door lets a Leper into house)

And there came a leper to him.

Leper: *(kneeling before Jesus)*
If You will, You can make me clean.

Jesus: I will. Be clean.

(MUSIC UP AND UNDER)

Chorus #1: And as soon as Jesus had spoken, the leprosy departed from him, and he was made clean. And after Jesus had given him a straight commandment, He sent him away,

Jesus: *(calling after the Leper from door SL)*
See you say nothing to any man, but go and show yourself to the Priest, and offer for your cleansing those things which Moses commanded, for a testimonial to them!

(During the next speech, the Leper crosses behind risers, then reappears on the other side and begins "telling" others on risers in excited motions.)

Chorus #1: *(still DSR)* But when he had departed, he began to tell many things, so that Jesus could no more openly enter into the city, but was outside in desert places. And they came to Him from every quarter. *(exit SR)*

(CROWD SFX UP SLOWLY, *as Jesus and disciples move into another "house" CS)*

Chorus #2: *(DSL)* After a few days, He entered into Capernaum again, and word spread that He was in the house. And many gathered together, insomuch that the places outside the door could not receive anymore. And He preached the word to them.

(SFX - CHOPPING *as everyone looks up)*

Chorus #2: And there came to him one sick of the palsy carried by four men. And because they could not come near to Him for the multitude, they uncovered the roof of the house where he was. And when they had broken it open, they let down the bed wherein the sick man lay.

(Jesus and the others make way for four people carrying another down from the risers to CS. They could also simply hold the person by the arms and let them lay them down on their own if this is too difficult)

Chorus #2: Now when Jesus saw their faith, He said to the sick man,

Jesus: *(kneeling, softly)* Son, your sins are forgiven you.

Chorus #2: And there were certain of the Scribes sitting there, and reasoning in their hearts,

Scribe #1: Why does this man speak such blasphemies?

Scribe #2: Who can forgive sins, but God only?

Chorus #2: And immediately, Jesus perceived their thoughts in His Spirit,

Jesus: Why do you reason these things in your hearts? Which is easier; to say to the sick of the palsy, 'Your sins are forgiven you?' or to say, 'Arise, take up your bed, and walk?' But that you may know that the Son of Man has authority in earth to forgive sins...

(standing, to the sick man, boldly)
Arise! Take up your bed and walk to your own house.

Chapter 2 (2:12-3:4)

*(begin **WTB_Mark02u_mix**)*

***(MUSIC SWELLS UP AND UNDER WITH CROWD NOISE**, then man gets up and slowly exits SR as he receives mimed "congratulations" of the crowd)*

Chorus #2: And by and by he arose, and took up his bed, and went forth before them all. And they were all amazed, and glorified God, saying, *(exit)*

Scribe #2: We never saw such a thing!

***(MUSIC CHANGE**. Jesus, who has followed everyone SR, turns around with Peter, James, John, Andrew and Chorus #3 and begins walking back CS toward Matthew, who is sitting on the floor. Chorus #3 peels off and moves DSR)*

Chorus #3: Then Jesus went forth again toward the sea, and all the people followed Him. And He taught them. And as He passed by, he saw Levi, the son of Alphaeus, sit at the tax collector's table.

Jesus: *(turning back, after he has passed him)* Follow me.

Chorus #3: *(amazed at how quickly Levi makes his decision)* And he arose and followed Him!

(during next speech, Jesus' group joins with several from the risers to enter Matthew's "house" DSL. there are perhaps 10 or 12 in all)

Chorus #3: And it came to pass, as Jesus sat at table in his house, many tax collectors and sinners sat at table also with Jesus and His disciples. For there were many of them that followed Him. And when the Scribes and Pharisees saw Him eat with the tax collectors and sinners, they said to His disciples,

(MUSIC OUT)

Pharisee #1: *(speaking with a couple of disciples who have stepped outside the house)*

How is it, that He eats and drinks with them?

Jesus: *(hearing or perceiving them from inside and speaking loudly so they can hear, but not looking toward them at all, rather at his disciples inside)* The healthy have no need of the Physician, but the sick. I came not to call the righteous, but the sinners to repentance.

Chorus #3: And the disciples of John and the Pharisees fasted, and came and said to Him,

Disciple: *(from inside house)* Why do the disciples of John, and of the Pharisees fast, and not Your disciples?

Jesus: Can the children of the marriage chamber fast while the Bridegroom is with them? As long as they have the Bridegroom with them, they cannot fast. But the days will come, when the Bridegroom shall be taken from them, and then shall they fast in those days. Also no man sows a piece of new cloth in an old garment, or else the new piece that fills it up takes away somewhat from the old, and the breach is worse.

Likewise, no man puts new wine into old vessels, or else the new wine breaks the vessels, and the wine runs out, and the vessels are lost. But new wine must be put into new vessels.

(during the next speech, everyone returns to risers, which now become the synagogue, except Jesus' group, who moves CS as the man with the withered hand joins them there. Chorus #1 peels off from that group and moves DSL)

Chorus #1: And He entered again into the Synagogue. And there was a man which had a withered hand. And they watched Him, whether He would heal him on the Sabbath day, that they might accuse Him.

Jesus: Arise! Stand in front of the crowd.
(to the crowd)
Is it lawful to do a good deed on the Sabbath day, or to do evil!? To save the life, or to kill!?

Chapter 3 (3:4-35)

*(begin **WTB_Mark03u_mix**)*

Chorus #1: But they held their peace.

Then He looked at all of them angrily, mourning also for the hardness of their hearts.

Jesus: *(to the man)* Stretch forth your hand.

*(pause, then **MUSIC UP AND UNDER, WITH CROWD SFX**)*

Chorus #1: And he stretched it out. And his hand was restored, as whole as the other. *(exit)*

*(**MUSIC CHANGE TO TRIBAL DURGE W/CROWD UNDERNEATH** as everyone, including Chorus #1, follows Jesus off SR and Chorus #2 moves DSL)*

Chorus #2: And the Pharisees departed, and immediately gathered a council with the Herodians against Jesus, that they might destroy Him.

Chorus #3: *(DSR)* But Jesus withdrew with His disciples to the sea. And a great multitude followed Him from Galilee, and from Judea, and from Jerusalem, and from Idumea, and beyond Jordan.

Chorus #2: And they that dwelled about Tyre and Sidon, when they had heard what great things He did, came to Him in great number.

Chorus #3: And He commanded His disciples, that a little ship should wait for Him, because of the multitude, lest they should throng Him. For He had healed many, so that they pressed upon Him to touch Him, as many as had plagues.

Chorus #2: And when the unclean spirits saw Him, they fell down before Him, saying, "You are the Son of God!" And He sharply rebuked them, that they should not tell who He was.

*(**MUSIC CHANGE**. During the next six lines, Jesus enters SR with crowd and crosses to CS. As he calls each Apostle, he lays hands upon him and each takes a seat on the ground in a semi-circle around him. Everyone else moves back up on risers)*

Chorus #3: *(still DSR)* Then Jesus went up into a mountain, and called to Him whom He would, and they came to Him.

Chorus #2: *(still DSL)* And He appointed twelve, that they should be with Him, and that He might send them to preach. And that they might have power to heal sicknesses, and to cast out demons.

Chorus #3: And the first was Simon, and He named Simon, Peter. Then James the son of Zebedee, and John James' brother (and surnamed them Boanerges, which is, The Sons of Thunder.)

Chorus #2: And Andrew, and Philip, and Bartholomew.

Chorus #3: And Matthew, and Thomas, and James the son of Alphaeus. *(exit)*

Chorus #2: And Thaddaeus, and Simon the Canaanite, and Judas Iscariot, who also betrayed Him. And they came home.

(MUSIC OUT, CROWD SFX UP AND OUT)

Chorus #1: *(DSR)* And the multitude assembled again, so that they could not even eat. And when His kinsfolk heard of it, they went out to lay hold of Him. For they said that He was beside Himself. And the Scribes which came down from Jerusalem, said, "He has Beelzebub! And through the prince of the demons He casts out demons!" But Jesus called them to Himself, and said to them in parables,

Jesus: *(DCS, to audience)* How can Satan drive out Satan? For if a kingdom be divided against itself, that kingdom cannot stand. Or if a house be divided against itself, that house cannot continue.

So if Satan make insurrection against himself, and be divided, he cannot endure, but is at an end. No man can enter into a strong man's house, and take away his goods, except he first bind that strong man, and then spoil his house. Truly I say to you, all sins shall be forgiven the children of men, and blasphemies. But he that blasphemes against the Holy Spirit, shall never have forgiveness, but is culpable of eternal damnation.

Chorus #1: Jesus said this because they said, He had an unclean spirit. *(exit)*

(during next speech, Mother and brothers enter SL and stop at "door" SL. Peter then enters "house"- no need to mime door open/close. This needs to happen rather quickly)

Then came His brothers and mother and stood outside, and sent for Him. And the people sitting near Him said to Him,

Peter: Behold, Your mother, and Your brothers seek for You outside.

Jesus: *(seated, CS)* Who is My mother and My brother?

(looking at those seated around Him)

Behold My mother and My brothers. For whoever does the will of God, he is My brother, My sister, and My mother.

Chapter 4 (4:1-20,26-29,35-41)

*(Begin **WTB_Mark04u_mix**. Jesus stands CS with The 12 seated on the floor around him in a boat-shaped pattern. Everyone else moves down from the risers and sits on the "shore" SR)*

Chorus #2: *(DSL)* And Jesus began again to teach by the seaside, and there gathered to Him a great multitude, so that He entered into a ship, and sat in the sea, and all the people were by the seaside on the land. And He taught them many things in parables.

(SFX - BOAT OARS BEING PUT AWAY)

Jesus: Hear now! Behold, there went out a sower to sow. And it came to pass as he sowed, that some fell by the wayside, and the birds came, and devoured it up. And some fell on stony ground, and by and by sprang up, because it had not depth of earth. But as soon as the Sun was up, it was burnt up, and because it had not root, it withered away. And some fell among the thorns, and the thorns grew up, and choked it, so that it gave no fruit. Some again fell in good ground, and did yield fruit that sprung up, and grew, and it brought forth, some thirtyfold, some sixtyfold, and some a hundredfold. He that has ears to hear, let him hear.

*(**MUSICAL INTERLUDE UP AND UNDER** while all but The 12 move back up on risers)*

Chorus #2: And when He was alone, they that were with Him asked Him about the parable. *(exit)*

(MUSIC OUT)

Jesus: *(still CS, with The 12 in the "boat")*
To you it is given to know the mystery of the kingdom of God. But to them that are outside, all things are done in parables. That they seeing, may see and not discern; and they hearing, may hear and not understand. Or else at any time they might turn, and their sins would be forgiven them.
Do you not perceive this parable? How then should you understand all other parables? The sower sows the word. And these are they that receive the seed by the wayside, in whom the word is sown. But when they have heard it, Satan comes immediately, and takes away the word that was sown in their hearts. And likewise they that receive the seed in stony ground are they which, when they have heard the word, immediately receive it with gladness. Yet have they no root in themselves, and endure but a time. For when trouble and persecution arise for the word, immediately they are put off. Also they that receive the seed among the thorns, are such as hear the word, but the cares of this world, and the deceitfulness of riches, and the lusts of other things enter in, and choke the word, and it is unfruitful. But they that have received seed in good ground, are they that hear the word, and receive it, and bring forth fruit: one corn thirty, another sixty, and some a hundred. So is the kingdom of God. A man scatters seed on the ground. Night and day, whether he sleeps or gets up, the seed sprouts and grows, though he does not know how. All by itself the soil produces grain —first the stalk, then the head, then the full kernel in the head. As soon as the grain is ripe, he puts the sickle to it, because the harvest has come.

(MUSIC UP AND UNDER)

Chorus #3: *(DSL)* Now the same day when evening came, Jesus said to them,

Jesus: Let us pass over unto the other side.

Chorus #3: And they left the multitude, and took Him as He was in the ship, and there was also with Him other little ships.

(SFX - WIND/STORM)

And there arose a great storm of wind, and the waves dashed into the ship, so that it was now full. And Jesus was in the stern asleep on a pillow. And they awoke Him,

Simon Zealot: Master, don't you care if we perish?!

Chorus #3: And he rose up, and rebuked the wind, and sea,

Jesus: Peace! And be still!

*(**WIND/STORM SFX END ABRUPTLY**, at precisely the same instant, The 12 falls to the ground, leaving Jesus standing alone. **DISCIPLES BEGIN TALKING IN AMAZEMENT**)*

Chorus #3: So the wind ceased. And it was a great calm.

Jesus: Why are you so fearful? How is it that you have no faith?

Chorus #3: And they feared exceedingly, and said one to another, *(exit)*

James: Who is this, that both the wind and sea obey him?

Chapter 5 (5:1-17_6:7-13,30)

*(Begin **WTB_Mark05u_mix**)*

Chorus #1: *(DSR)* And they came over to the other side of the sea, into the country of the Gadarenes. And when Jesus had come out of the ship, there met Him incontinently out of the graves, a man who had an unclean spirit.
The man dwelt among the graves, and no man could bind him, not even with chains. For if anyone tried, he would pluck the chains apart and break the fetters in pieces. So no one could tame him.
And always, both night and day he cried in the mountains, and in the graves, and struck himself with stones.
And when he saw Jesus afar off, he ran and worshiped him,

(Jesus and The 12 enter SR and Legion enters SL and meets them CS)

(MUSIC OUT, DEMONIC SFX UP AND UNDER)

Legion: *(writhing on his knees)* What have I to do with You, Jesus the Son of the most High God? Swear to me by God that You will not torment me!

Jesus: *(standing above him)* Come out of the man, you unclean spirit! What is your name?

Legion: My name is Legion: for we are many.

Chorus #1: And the demon prayed to Jesus that He would not send them away out of the country.

(OMINOUS CHORAL MUSIC ALSO BUILDS UNDERNEATH)

Now there was there in the mountains a great heard of pigs, feeding. And all the demons begged Jesus, saying,

Legion: *(still on the ground)* Send us into the pigs, that we may enter into them!

(SFX - PIGS DESCENDING INTO THE LAKE AND DROWNING UNDERNEATH *as Legion rises and runs off SL with the crowd following, leaving Jesus and The 12 CS)*

Chorus #1: And Jesus gave them leave. Then the unclean spirits went out and entered into the pigs, and the herd ran headlong from the high bank into the sea. And there were about two thousand pigs. And they were choked up in the sea. *(exit)*

(MUSIC AND PIG SFX FADE OUT, THEN MUSIC AND CROWD SFX UP AND UNDER)

Chorus #2: *(DSL)* And the swineherds fled, and told about it in the city, and in the country. And they came out to see what it was that was done. And they came to Jesus, and saw him that had been possessed with the demon, and had the legion, sit both clothed, and in his right mind. And they were afraid.

And they that saw it, told them what was done to him that was possessed with the demon, and about the pigs. Then they began to ask Him to depart from their coasts.

(SAME MUSIC CONTINUES UNDERNEATH. During the next speech, Jesus begins to send The 12 offstage in pairs in various directions.)

Chorus #2: And He called to Himself the twelve, and began to send them forth two and two, and gave them power over unclean spirits.
And commanded them that they should take nothing for their journey, except a staff only - not a bag, nor bread, nor money in their belts. But that they should wear sandals and that they should not put on two coats.

Jesus: *(pausing at about the 4th pair, with his hands on them, and then sending the rest out in all directions during this speech)*

Whatever house you shall enter into, stay there until you depart from that town. And whomever shall not receive you, nor hear you, when you depart from there, shake off the dust that is under your feet, for a witness to them. Truly I say to you, it shall be easier for Sodom or Gomorrah at the day of Judgment than for that city.

Chorus #2: *(During this speech, the 12 rejoin Jesus from all points offstage, with a crowd of at least 8-10 following as well. If the stage is big enough, the entire cast should be surrounding them.)*

And they went out and preached, that all should repent. And they cast out many demons. And they anointed many that were sick with oil, and healed them. And the Apostles gathered themselves together to Jesus, and told Him all things, both what they had done, and what they had taught. *(exit)*

Chapter 6 (6:31-56)

*(music out, begin **WTB_Mark06u_mix**)*

Jesus: Come away into the wilderness and rest a while.

(Jesus and The 12 move DSR, crowd remains CS. Chorus #3 peels away from crowd and moves DSL)

Chorus #3: For there were many comers and goers, and they had not had a chance to eat.
So they went by ship out of the way into a desert place. But the people saw them when they departed, and many knew Jesus, and ran after them out of all cities, and got to the desert place before them.

(Jesus moves CS with The 12 and mimes a few simple hand gestures to the crowd, then turns DCS with Philip and Andrew for the ensuing scene)

Then Jesus went out, and saw a great multitude, and had compassion on them, because they were like sheep which had no shepherd: and he began to teach them many things. And when the day was now far spent, His disciples came to Him.

Philip: This is a desert place, and now the day is old. Let them depart, that they may go into the country and towns and buy bread, for they have nothing to eat.

Chorus #3: But Jesus answered, *(exit)*

Jesus: YOU give them something to eat.

Andrew: Shall we go and buy two hundred pennies worth of bread and give that to them to eat?

Jesus: How many loaves do you have?

Andrew: Five, and two fishes.

(UPLIFTING CHORAL MUSIC UP AND UNDER, as crowd sits UCS. During the next 3 speeches, the 12 mime distributing loaves first, and then the fish)

Chorus #1: *(DSR)* So he commanded them to make them all sit down in groups upon the green grass. Then they sat down by rows, by hundreds, and by 50s. And he took the five loaves, and the two fishes, and looked up to heaven, and gave thanks, and broke the loaves, and gave them to his disciples to set before them, and the two fishes he divided among them all.

(during the first part of the next speech, crowd rises and returns to risers)

So they did all eat, and were satisfied. And they took up twelve baskets full of the fragments, and of the fishes. And they that had eaten were about five thousand men.
And immediately he caused his disciples to go into the ship and go before Him to the other side, to Bethsaida, while He sent away the people.

(MUSIC OUT)

Then as soon as He had sent them away, He departed into a mountain to pray. *(exit)*

(STORM SFX)

Chorus #1: *(The 12 appear DSL in the "boat")*
And when evening came, the ship was in the midst of the sea and Jesus alone on the land. And He saw them troubled in rowing, for the wind was contrary unto them.

(Jesus has left the stage by now)

And about the fourth watch of the night, He came to them, walking on the sea, and would have passed by them.

(The 12 look out over the audience as if seeing Jesus walking on the water)

And when they saw Him walking upon the sea, they thought it was a spirit, and cried out. For they all saw Him, and were very afraid. But He said to them,

Jesus: *(into offstage mic)* Be of good comfort! It is I! Be not afraid!

Chorus #1: Then He went up to them into the ship, and the wind ceased.

*(**STORM SFX OUT QUICKLY** along with all stage lights. If no lights are available, have everyone freeze in amazement, looking out toward the audience)*

Chorus #1: And they were much more amazed, and marveled. For they had not considered *the* matter of the loaves, because their hearts were hardened. *(exit)*

*(**TRIUMPHANT MUSIC UP AND UNDER**)*

Chorus #2: *(entering SR and moving DSR. The next 3 speeches are narration only)*

And they came over, and went into the land of Gennesaret.
So when they came out of the ship, immediately they knew Him, and ran throughout all that region and began to carry back and forth in couches all that were sick, where they heard that He was. And wherever He entered into towns, or cities, or villages, they laid their sick in the streets, and begged Him to touch at the least the edge of His garment. And as many as touched Him, were made whole. *(exit)*

(MUSIC OUT)

Chapter 7 (7:1-23)

*(Begin **WTB_Mark07u_mix**)*

Chorus #3: *(DSL)* Then gathered to Him the Pharisees and certain of the Scribes which came from Jerusalem. And when they saw some of His disciples eat meat with common hands - that is to say, unwashed - they complained. For the Pharisees, and all the Jews, do not eat unless they wash their hands, holding to the traditions of the Elders.

Chorus #1: *(moving DCS)* And when they come from the market, they do not eat until they have washed. And there are many other things which they have taken upon themselves to observe, as the washing of cups, and pots, and of brazen vessels, and of beds. Then asked the Pharisees and Scribes, *(both Choruses exit)*

(this scene takes place DSR)

Pharisee: Why don't your disciples walk according to the tradition of the Elders, and eat meat with unwashed hands?

Jesus: Surely Isaiah has prophesied well of you, hypocrites,

(CROWD MURMURING SFX)

as it is written,

'This people honors Me with their lips, but their heart is far away from Me. But they worship Me in vain, teaching doctrines and commandments of men.'

For you lay the Commandments of God apart, and observe the tradition of men, as the washing of pots and of cups, and of many other such things. You intentionally reject the commandment of God, that you may observe your own tradition. For Moses said,

'Honor your father and your mother.'
and
'Whoever shall speak evil of father or mother, let him die the death.'

But you say,

'If a man says to his father or mother, 'Corban', that is, 'The gift that I once offered for you shall now be devoted to God, that man shall be free from his obligation.'

So you no longer require him to do anything for his father or his mother. Making the word of God of no authority, by your tradition, which you have ordained. And you do many other such things.

(now to the whole crowd)

Hear Me now, and understand!

There is nothing outside a man that can defile him, when it enters into him. But the things which proceed out of him, are they which defile the man.

If any have ears to hear, let him hear!

(MUSIC UP AND UNDER, THEN FIRE CRACKLING SFX, *as Jesus and The 12 move DCS and sit in a semi-circle, with Jesus in the center, facing the audience while talking to them)*

Chorus #2: *(DSL)* And when He came into a house, away from the people, His disciples asked Him about the parable.

Jesus: What? Are you without understanding also? Do you not know that whatever thing from outside enters into a man, cannot defile him, because it entered not into his heart, but into the belly, and goes out into the draught which is the purging of all meats? *(that last line is meant as a joke)*
That which comes out of man, that defiles man. For from within, even out of the heart of men, proceed evil thoughts, adulteries, fornications, murders, thefts, covetousness, wickedness, deceit, uncleanliness, a wicked eye, backbiting, pride, foolishness. All these evil things come from within, and defile a man.

Chapter 8 (8:22-38_9:1)

*(**Begin WTB_Mark08u_mix.** As Jesus and the 12 move around behind the SL side of the risers, Chorus #3 begins speaking from the center of the risers as he slowly moves DSL)*

Chorus #3: And He came to Bethsaida, and they brought a blind man to Him, and asked Him to touch him.

(Jesus and The 12 re-emerge with the Blind Man from behind the SR side of the risers and move DSR.)

Then He took the blind man by the hand, and led him out of the town, and spit in his eyes, and put His hands upon him, and asked him, if he saw anything. And he looked up, and said,

Blind Man: I see men walking like trees.

(WONDROUS MUSIC UP AND UNDER)

Chorus #3: After that, He put his hands on his eyes again, and made him look again. And his sight was restored. And he saw every man clearly. And Jesus sent him home to his house. *(exit)*

(Blind Man exits USR as Jesus calls after him.)

Jesus: Don't go into the town, nor tell it to anyone in the town!

*(**MUSIC OUT.** During the next line, Chorus #1 peels off from The 12 and moves DSR, while they continue SL with Jesus)*

Chorus #1: *(DSR)* And Jesus went out with His disciples into the towns of Caesarea Philippi. And along the way He asked his disciples,

Jesus: Whom do men say that I am?

John: Some say, John Baptist.

James: And some, Elijah.

Bartholemew: And some, one of the Prophets.

Jesus: *(stopping)* But whom do YOU say that I am?

(pause)

Peter: You are that Christ.

***(SLIGHTLY OMINOUS MUSIC UP AND UNDER** as Jesus and The 12 freeze DSL)*

Chorus #1: And Jesus sharply charged them that concerning Him they should tell no man.
Then He began to teach them that the Son of Man must suffer many things. And that He would be rejected by the Elders, and by the high Priests, and by the Scribes. And that He would be slain. And that within three days, He would rise again. And he spoke that thing boldly.

Then Peter took Him aside, and began to rebuke Him. And Jesus turned back and looked at His disciples, and rebuked Peter, *(exit)*

Jesus: *(crossing DCS and speaking toward the audience, as The 12 slowly move center and form another semi-circle behind him)*

27

Get behind me, Satan! For you do not understand the things that are of God, but the things that are of men!

(moving freely among The 12, speaking to everyone, both them and the audience)

Whoever will follow me, let him forsake himself, and take up his cross, and follow Me. For whoever will save his life, shall lose it. But whoever shall lose his life for My sake and the Gospel's, he shall save it. For what shall it profit a man, though he should win the whole world, if he lose his soul? Or what exchange shall a man give for his soul?

For whoever shall be ashamed of Me, and of My words among this adulterous and sinful generation, of him shall the Son of Man be ashamed also, when He comes in the glory of His Father with the holy Angels.

Chapter 9 (9:1-13_31-32)

(back to Disciples only)

Jesus: Truly I say to you, that there be some of them that stand here which shall not taste of death till they have seen the kingdom of God come with power.

(Begin WTB_Mark09u_mix. *Jesus moves to first riser UCS as everyone else parts, moving offstage, except for Peter, James and John, who stand on either side of Him)*

Chorus #2: *(DSL)* And six days later, Jesus took with Him Peter and James and John, and carried them up into a high mountain, out of the way, alone.

(ETHEREAL MUSIC AND TRANSFIGURATION SFX as Jesus moves to top riser alone)

And Jesus was transfigured before them.

Chorus #3: *(DSR)* And His clothing shined, and was very white as snow, whiter than anyone in the world could bleach them.

(During the next speech, Jesus remains alone on the top step. The audience does not see Elijah and Moses—only the 3 Disciples. Perhaps Jesus could raise his arms to a horizontal position, but nothing more physically demonstrative than that.)

Chorus #2: And there appeared to them Elijah with Moses, and they were talking with Jesus. Then Peter said to Jesus,

Peter: *(moving to second step)* Master, it is good for us to be here. Let us make three tabernacles, one for You, and one for Moses, and one for Elijah.

Chorus #3: Yet he knew not what he said: for they were afraid. And there was a cloud that shadowed them. And a voice came out of the cloud, saying,

God: *(RECORDED)* This is my beloved Son. Hear Him.

Chorus #2: And suddenly they looked around, and saw no more any man, except for Jesus, with them.

(PENSIVE MUSIC UP AND UNDER, as Peter, James, John and Jesus slowly move down from the risers DCS during the next three lines, with Jesus making a few subtle gestures indicating his desire for discretion - such as a gentle "shh" sign)

And as they came down from the mountain, He charged them that they should tell no man what they had seen until the Son of man were risen from the dead again.

Chorus #3: So they kept that matter to themselves, and asked only of each other what the 'rising from the dead again' should mean.

(MUSIC OUT)

Then they asked Jesus, saying,

James: Why do the Scribes say that Elijah must come first?

Jesus: Elijah truly shall come first, and restore all things. And as it is written of the Son of Man; He must suffer many things, and be rejected. But I say to you that Elijah has come, and they have done to him whatsoever they would. As it is written of him.

The Son of man shall be delivered into the hands of men, and they shall kill Him. But after He is killed, He shall rise again the third day.

(SHORT MUSIC BED UP AND UNDER)

Chorus #2: But they understood not that saying, and were afraid to ask Him.

Chapter 10 (10:13-34)

*(**Begin WTB_Mark10u_mix.** The 12 cross DCS in front of Jesus, looking menacingly into audience)*

Chorus #3: Then they brought little children to Him, that He should touch them, and His disciples rebuked those that brought them. But when Jesus saw it, He was displeased, and said to them,

Jesus: *(breaking through The 12 and speaking to them while kneeling and looking out at the audience as if they are the children)*

Let the little children come to Me, and forbid them not. For of such is the kingdom of God. Truly I say to you, whoever shall not receive the kingdom of God as a little child, he shall not enter therein.

(Jesus mimes placing his arms around children)

Chorus #2: And He took them up in His arms, and put His hands on them, and blessed them.

(Jesus stands as the Rich Man enters SR)

And when He had gone a little further, there came one running, and knelt down to Him, and asked Him,

Rich Man: Good Master, what shall I do, that I may possess eternal life?

Jesus: Why do you call me good? There is none good but one, even God. You know the commandments. You shall not commit adultery. You shall not kill. You shall not steal. You shall not bear false witness. You shall hurt no man. Honor your father and mother.

Rich Man: *(rises in excitement)* Master, all these things have I observed from my youth!

Chorus #3: And Jesus looked at him, and loved him,

Jesus: One thing you lack. Go and sell all that you have, and give it to the poor, and you shall have treasure in heaven. And come, follow me, and take up the cross.

(Rich Man turns and exits slowly as Chorus #2 continues)

Chorus #2: But the rich man was sad at that saying, and went away sorrowful. For he had great possessions.

Jesus: *(watching man leave)* How hard it is for they who have riches to enter into the kingdom of God!

Chorus #3: And His disciples were afraid at His words.

Jesus: *(to disciples)* Children, how hard is it for them that trust in riches, to enter into the kingdom of God! It is easier for a camel to go through the eye of a needle, than for a rich man to enter into the kingdom of God.

Chorus #2: And they were much more astonished.

Thomas: *(to the other disciples)* Who then can be saved?

(THE OTHER DISCIPLES RESPOND AND BEGIN TO MURMUR QUIETLY AMONG THEMSELVES *before Jesus interrupts)*

Jesus: With men it is impossible, but not with God. For with God, all things are possible.

Peter: Lo, we have left all, and have followed You.

Jesus: Truly I say to you, there is no man that has left house, or brothers, or sisters, or father, or mother, or wife, or children, or lands for My sake and the Gospels, who shall not receive a hundredfold as much, now at this present time, houses, and brothers, and sisters, and mothers, and children, and lands, with persecutions, and in the world to come, eternal life. But many *that are* first, shall be last, and the last, first.

*(FREEZE as **"WIND" UNDERSCORE GOES SILENT**. before **MUSIC BEGINS AGAIN UNDERNEATH**. If a BLACKOUT is possible, these last two lines of Act 1 should be spoken in the dark.)*

Chorus #1: *(from risers)* And as they were going up to Jerusalem, Jesus went before them. And they were troubled and afraid. And Jesus took the twelve again and began to tell them what things would happen to him, saying,

Jesus: *(DCS, to audience)* Behold, we go up to Jerusalem, and the Son of Man shall be delivered to the high Priests and to the Scribes. And they shall condemn Him to death. And shall deliver Him to the Gentiles. And they shall mock Him, and scourge Him, and spit upon Him, and kill Him. But the third day He shall rise again.

END ACT 1

ACT 2

Chapter 11 (11:1-11,15-18,27-33)

(Begin WTB_Mark11_12u_mix. All dialogue until Chorus #3's first line is spoken in blackout into offstage mics.)

Chorus #1: And when they came near to Jerusalem, to Bethpage and Bethany, to the mount of Olives, Jesus sent forth two of His disciples.

Jesus: Go into the next town, and as soon as you enter into it, you shall find a colt tied, whereon never man sat. Loosen him, and bring him. And if any man say to you, 'Why do you do this?' Say that the Lord has need of him. And immediately he will let you take him.

Chorus #1: And they went on their way, and found a colt, tied by the door, outside, in a place where two ways met. And they loosened him.

Villager: Hey, what are you doing?

Chorus #1: And they answered as Jesus had commanded them. And they let them go.

Chorus #2: And they brought the colt to Jesus, and cast their garments on him, and Jesus sat on him.

(CROWD SFX SWELL)

And many spread their garments in the way. Others cut down branches off the trees, and strew them in the way. And they that went before, and they that followed, cried out!

Worshiper #1: Hosanna! Blessed be He that comes in the Name of the Lord!

Worshiper #2: Blessed be the kingdom that comes in the Name of the Lord of our father David!

Worshiper #3: Hosanna, O You Who are in the highest heavens!

(lights up on Chorus #3)

Chorus #3: *(DSR)* So Jesus entered into Jerusalem, and into the Temple. And when He had looked about on all things, He went forth to Bethany with the twelve.

Chorus #1: *(DSL)* And the next day, Jesus went into the Temple, ...

(SILENCE. THEN CRASHING WOOD SFX)

Chorus #3: And began to cast out them that sold and bought in the Temple. And overthrew the tables of the money changers, and the seats of them that sold doves.

Chorus #1: Neither would He let anyone carry merchandise through the Temple. And He taught them.

Jesus: *(enters and crosses DCS quickly, alone. He is very animated and urgent, speaking to everyone all around him, as if in the very center of the crowded Temple. Think angry parent, not contemptuous, more disappointed and almost pleading. He has taught them this before.)*

Is it not written, 'My house shall be called the house of prayer to all nations'?! But you have made it a den of thieves!

Chorus #1: And the Scribes and high Priests heard it, and sought how to destroy Him. For they feared Him. Because the whole multitude was astonished at His doctrine.

(SLIGHTLY OMINOUS PIANO TRANSITION UNDERNEATH)

Chorus #3: But when evening came, Jesus went out of the city. And in the morning they came again to Jerusalem: and as He walked in the Temple, there came to Him the high Priests, and the Scribes, and the Elders.

(2 Elders enter SL and speak with Jesus DSL)

Elder #1: By what authority do You do these things? And who gave You this authority, that You should do these things?

Jesus: I will also ask you a certain thing. Answer Me, and I will tell you by what authority I do these things. The baptism of John, was it from heaven, or of men? Answer Me.

(the elders move away, whispering in conference with each other)

Elder #1: If we say, 'From heaven',He will say, 'Why then did you not believe Him?'

Elder #2: But if we say, 'Of men', we fear the people.

Chorus #3: For all men counted John as a Prophet indeed.

Elder #1: *(back to Jesus)* We cannot tell!

(Jesus takes one step to Elders and speaks softly but not in a whisper)

Jesus: Neither will I tell you by what authority I do these things.

Chapter 12 (12:28-34)

(action moves back CS as the Old Scribe enters SR and takes the place of the Elders, who return to risers. Chorus #2 appears DSL)

Chorus #2: Then came one of the Scribes that had heard them disputing together, and had perceived that Jesus had answered them well.

Old Scribe : Which is the first commandment of all?

Jesus: The first of all the commandments is, 'Hear, Israel, The Lord our God is the only Lord. You shall therefore love the Lord your God with all your heart, and with all your soul, and with all your mind, and with all your strength.' This is the first commandment. And the second is like it, 'You shall love your neighbor as yourself.' There is no other commandment greater than these.

(SLIGHT COMMOTION AMONG THE CROWD)

Old Scribe: Well, Master. You have said the truth; that there is one God. And that there is none but He. And to love Him with all the heart, and with all the understanding, and with all the soul, and with all the strength, and to love his neighbor as himself, is more than all whole burnt offerings and sacrifices.

(still more commotion, as the Scribe has surprised even himself with his words)

Jesus: *(crosses to him, whispers)*
You are not far from the kingdom of God.

(PIANO MUSIC STING UNDERNEATH)

Chorus #2: And no man after that dared to ask Him any question.

Chapter 13 (13:1-20,24-37)

*(Begin **WTB_Mark13u_mix**)*

Chorus #1: *(DSR. During this speech, Jesus moves DCS and The 12 move into the House a bit as if admiring the buildings of Jerusalem. Peter, James, John and Andrew - aka "The 4" - remain onstage with Jesus)*

Then Jesus and His disciples went out of the Temple.

Thaddaeus: *(amazed)* Master, see what manner stones, and what manner buildings are here!

Jesus: *(also looking)* See these great buildings? There shall not be left one stone upon a stone, that shall not be thrown down.

*(**MUSICAL TRANSITION UNDER** as The 12 sit where they are in the aisles of the House and onstage)*

Chorus #1: And as Jesus sat on the mount of Olives, next to the Temple, Peter, and James, and John, and Andrew asked him secretly, *(exit)*

Andrew: *(seated)* Tell us, when shall these things be?

Peter: And what shall be the sign when all these things shall be fulfilled?

(AMBIENT DRAMATIC MUSIC BUILDS VERY SLOWLY DURING THIS SPEECH)

Jesus: *(kneeling in the center of The 4)* Take heed lest any man deceive you. For many shall come in My Name, saying, 'I am Christ', and shall deceive many.

Furthermore, when you shall hear of wars, and rumors of wars, be not troubled. For such things must be. But the end shall not be yet.

(rises, begins to move CS slowly, speaking to the entire theatre) For nation shall rise against nation, and kingdom against kingdom. And there shall be earthquakes in diverse quarters.

(back to The 4) And there shall be famine and trouble. These are the beginnings of sorrows.

(now speaking to everyone again)

But take heed to yourselves. For they shall deliver you up to the Councils, and to the Synagogues. You shall be beaten, and brought before rulers and kings for My sake, for a testimonial to them. And the Gospel must first be published among all nations.

(slight pause)

But when they deliver you up, be not careful before hand, neither study what you shall say, but what is given you at the same time, that speak. For it is not you that speak, but My Spirit.

(moves upstage toward first riser)

Yea, and the brother shall deliver the brother to death, and the father the son, and the children shall rise against their parents, and shall cause them to die. And you shall be hated of all men for my Name's sake. But whoever shall endure to the end, he shall be saved.

(ascends to first riser)

Moreover, when you shall see the abomination of desolation, spoken of by Daniel the Prophet, set where it ought not be, then let them that be in Judea, flee into the mountains. And let him that is upon the house, not come down into the house, neither enter therein, to fetch anything out of his house. And let him that is in the field, not turn back again to take his garment. Then woe shall be to them that are with child, and to them that give suck in those days.

(ascends to next step)

Pray therefore that your flight be not in the winter. For those days shall be such tribulation, as was not from the beginning of the creation which God created unto this time, neither shall be.

And except that the Lord had shortened those days, no flesh should be saved. But for the elect's sake, which He has chosen, He has shortened those days.

(ascends another step)

Moreover in those days, after that tribulation, the sun shall wax dark, and the moon shall not give her light. And the stars of heaven shall fall. And the powers which are in heaven, shall shake.

(should be at the top by now, speaking toward Heaven, quite joyously as if seeing a vision. During the next speech, the Disciples in the House stand and return to the stage.)

And then shall they see the Son of Man coming in the clouds with great power and glory. And He shall then send His Angels, and shall gather together His elect from the four winds, and from the utmost part of the earth to the utmost part of heaven.

(MUSIC ENDS. OUTDOOR SFX UP, BIRDS, BREEZE)

(Jesus descends the risers and meets all of the Disciples CS once again)

Now learn a parable of the fig tree. When her bough is yet tender, and it brings forth leaves, you know that summer is near. So in like manner, when you see these things come to pass, know that *the kingdom of God is near, even at the doors.*
Truly I say to you, that this generation shall not pass, till all these things be done. Heaven and earth shall pass away, but My words shall not pass away.

(these last lines are spoken back an forth between audience and The 12)

But of that day and hour knows no man, no, not the Angels which are in heaven, neither the Son himself, but the Father.

Take heed. Watch, and pray. For you know not when the master of the house will come; at evening, or at midnight, at the cock crowing, or in the dawning. Lest if he come suddenly, he should find you sleeping. And those things that I say to you, I say to all men.

(to audience) Watch.

Chapter 14 (All verses)

(Begin WTB_Mark14u_mix)

Chorus #2: *(DSR)* And two days before the feast of the Passover and of unleavened bread, the high Priests and Scribes sought how they might secretly take Jesus, and put Him to death.

High Priest: *(from risers)*
But...Not in the feast day, lest there be any rioting among the people!

(SFX – WOODEN UTENSILS CLANGING, ETC)

Chorus #2: *(as Jesus and The 12 enter and sit DSL)*

And when Jesus was in Bethany in the house of Simon the leper, as He was eating,

(woman descends from risers)

there came a woman with box of ointment, of Spikenard, very costly, and she broke the box, and poured it on Jesus' head.

(MURMURING SFX)

Therefore some disdained her among themselves.

Judas: To what end is this waste of ointment? For it might have been sold for more than a year's wages and the money given to the poor.

Chorus #2: And they murmured against her. *(exit)*

Jesus: Let her alone. Why does she trouble you? She has done a good work for Me. For he poor you will have with you always. And when you will you may do them good. But Me you shall not have always.

(crosses to Judas)

She has done what she could. She came beforehand to anoint My body to the burying. Truly I say to you, wherever this Gospel shall be preached throughout the whole world, this also that she has done shall be spoken of in remembrance of her.

(OMINOUS MUSIC UP AND UNDERNEATH)

Chorus #1: *(peels off from Disciples and moves DSL while they continue moving DSR with Jesus)*
Then Judas Iscariot, one of the twelve, went away to the high Priests, to betray Jesus to them. And when they heard it, they were glad, and promised that they would give him money. Therefore he sought how he might conveniently betray Jesus.

(MUSIC OUT, OUTDOOR AMBIENCE W/BIRDS UP)

Chorus #1: Now the first day of unleavened bread, when they sacrificed the Passover, Jesus' disciples came to Him,

John: Where will You have us go and prepare, that You may eat the Passover?

Chorus #1: Then He sent forth two of His disciples.

Jesus: Go into the city, and there shall a man meet you, bearing a pitcher of water. Follow him. And wherever he goes in, say to the good man of the house, 'My Master says, 'Where is the lodging where I shall eat the Passover with My disciples?' And he will show you an upper chamber which is large, trimmed and prepared. There make it ready for us.

(SHORT MUSICAL TRANSITION as 2 Disciples exit)

Chorus #1: So his disciples went into the city, and found everything as Jesus had said it would be, and made ready the Passover.

And in the evening, Jesus came with the twelve. And they sat at the table and ate. *(exit)*

(all on the floor, with Jesus CS)

Jesus: Truly I say to you, that one of you shall betray Me, who eats with me.

(VOCAL SFX OF CONFUSION, "WHAT!?", ETC...)

Thomas: Is it I?

Matthew: *(overlapping, sorrowful)* Is it I?

Jesus: *(pause)* It is one of the twelve that dips with me in the platter.

Truly the Son of Man goes His way, as it is written of Him. But woe be to that man by whom the Son of Man is betrayed. It had been good for that man if he had never been born.

(SOFT MAJESTIC MUSIC UP AND UNDER)

Chorus #3: *(DSR)* And as they ate, Jesus took the bread. And when He had given thanks, He broke it and gave it to them.

(Jesus pantomimes giving bread and wine to the left and right as He speaks)

Jesus: Take, eat, this is my body.

Chorus #3: Also He took the cup. And when He had given thanks, *(Jesus pantomimes passing cup to left)* He gave it to them. And they all drank of it.

Jesus: This is My blood of that New Testament, which is shed for many. *(receive cup back from left side and pass over to the right side while talking)* Truly I say to you, I will drink no more of the fruit of the vine until that day that I drink it new in the kingdom of God.

*(**MUSIC FADES, CRICKET SFX UP** as Jesus and The 12 move SL)*

Chorus #3: And when they had sung a Psalm, they went out to the mount of Olives.

Jesus: All of you shall desert me this night. For it is written, I will strike the shepherd, and the sheep shall be scattered.

(SFX-DISCIPLES MURMURING)
But after that I am risen, I will go into Galilee before you.

Chorus #3: And Peter said to Him,

Peter: Although all men should desert You, yet would not I!

Jesus: Truly I say to you this day, even in this night, before the cock crows twice, you shall deny Me three times.

Peter: If I should DIE with You, I will not deny You!

Chorus #3: And so said they all.

*(**OMINOUS TRANSITION MUSIC UP AND UNDER** as they all move CS)*

Chorus #3: Afterward, they came into a place named Gethsemane. *(exits)*

Jesus: Sit here, till I have prayed.

(Jesus moves DSR with Peter, James and John)

Chorus #2: *(DSL)* And He took with him Peter, and James, and John. And He began to be troubled, and in great heaviness.

Jesus: My soul is very heavy, even to the death. Stay here, and watch.

(Jesus moves further DSR alone)

Chorus #2: So He went forward a little, and fell down on the ground, and prayed, that if it were possible, that hour might pass from Him.

Jesus: Abba, Father, all things are possible for You. Take away this cup from Me. Nevertheless, not that I will, but that You will be done.

(Jesus rises and moves back to Peter, James and John)

Chorus #2: Then He returned, and found them sleeping, and said to Peter,

Jesus: *(waking him)* Simon!.. *(Peter stands)* Asleep? Could you not watch one hour?
Watch! And pray. So that you enter not into temptation. The spirit indeed is ready, but the flesh is weak.

***(SAD PIANO MUSIC UP AND UNDER.** Jesus freezes and Peter, James and John return to sleeping during the next speech)*

Chorus #2: And again He went away and prayed, and spoke the same words. And he returned, and found them asleep again. For their eyes were heavy. Neither knew they what they should answer Him.

And He came the third time, and said to them,

(MUSIC OUT)

Jesus: Sleep henceforth, and take your rest. It is enough. The hour is come. Behold, the Son of Man is delivered into the hands of sinners.

(MUSIC UP W/SFX OF JUDAS ARRIVING WITH ROMAN SOLDIERS)

Jesus: *(stepping DS, looking out at audience, but speaking to disciples)*

Rise up! Let us go! Lo, he that betrays me is at hand.

Chorus #2: And immediately while He yet spoke, came Judas, who was one of the twelve. And with him a great multitude with swords and clubs from the high Priests, and Scribes, and Elders.

And he that betrayed him, had given them a sign, saying,

(Judas appears FOH, instructing imaginary soldiers)

Judas Iscariot: Whomever I shall kiss, He it is. Take Him, and lead Him away safely.

(during the next line, Judas moves CS to Jesus, who turns slightly to meet his eyes)

Chorus #2: And as soon as he came, Judas went straight to Jesus.

Judas Iscariot: Hail, Master.

*(Judas kisses Jesus. Then **VOCAL SFX OF GUARDS SHOUTING** as Jesus is grabbed by the arms and held.)*

Chorus #2: Then they laid their hands on Him, and took Him. And one of them that stood by, drew out a sword, and struck a servant of the high Priest, and cut off his ear.

*(**SFX - GREAT COMMOTION AND SCREAMING** as Peter steps in front of Jesus CS and pantomimes cutting the guard's ear off)*

But Jesus answered, and said to them,

Jesus: *(breaks away from guards UC, steps in front of Peter, and holds guard's ear and head in His hands DCS, speaking directly to audience as if they were him)*

You come out as against a thief, with swords and with clubs, to take me. I was with you every day, teaching in the Temple, and you took Me not. But this is done that the Scriptures should be fulfilled.

*(pause, then **VOCAL SFX OF GUARDS "MOVE OFF!. GET BACK!, ETC"**)*

Chorus #2: Then they all deserted Him, and fled.

(PENSIVE MUSIC UP AND UNDER)

Chorus #3: *(beginning on risers and slowly moving DSR as the stage clears and actors return to risers)*

So they led Jesus away to the high Priest. And to Him came together all the high Priests, and the Elders, and the Scribes.

Chorus #1: *(DSL)* And Peter followed Him from far off, even into the hall of the high Priest, and sat with the servants, and warmed himself at the fire.

Chorus #3: And the high Priests, and all the Council, sought for witness against Jesus, to put Him to death. But found none. For many bore false witness against Him. *(exit)*

Trial Witness: *(from risers)* We heard him say, 'I will destroy this Temple made with hands, and within three days I will build another, made without hands.'

Chorus #1: But their accounts did not agree with each other.

(MUSIC OUT)

Then the high Priest stood up amongst them,

High Priest: *(from CS risers, toward audience)*
Answer You nothing? What is the matter that these bear witness against You?

(pause)

High Priest: Are You that Christ, the Son of...*(catches himself about to say God's name)*...the Blessed?

Jesus: *(DSR, also speaking out toward audience)*
I am He.

*(pause, **SFX – COMMOTION BUILDS DURING THE NEXT LINE**)*

And you shall see the Son of Man sit at the right hand of the power of *God, (emphasizes God's name as* **MUSIC AND CROWD COMMOTION SFX BUILD EVEN MORE**)

....and come in the clouds of heaven!

Chorus #1: *(still DSL)* Then the high Priest tore his clothes.

High Priest: What have we any more need of witnesses!? You have heard the blasphemy! What think you!?

Chorus #1: And they all condemned Him to be worthy of death.

*(**SFX – HECKLING, BEATING AND SPITTING**, as 2 Guards lead Jesus offstage, SR)*

And some began to spit at Him, and to cover His face, and to beat Him with fists, and to say to Him, "Prophesy!"

And the sergeants struck Him with their rods.

(HITTING AND CROWD SFX DIMINISH, BUT PIANO MUSIC STAYS UP, *as Peter appears DSR)*

And as Peter was beneath in the hall, there came to him one of the maids of the high Priest.

Maid #1: *(to Peter)* You were also with Jesus of Nazareth.

Peter: I know Him not. Neither do I understand what you're saying.

(crosses CS)

Chorus #1: Then he went out into the porch.

(ROOSTER CROWING SFX)

Chorus #1: And the cock crew.

(pause)

Then another maid saw him.

Maid #2: *(to bystanders with her)* This is one of them!

Chorus #1: But he denied it again. And soon after, they that stood by said again to Peter,

Man #1: *(crossing from SR to Peter, CS)* Surely you are one of them. For you are of Galilee, and your speech is like.

Chorus #1: And Peter began to curse, and swear.

Peter: *(crossing DSR)* I know not this Man of whom you speak!

(ROOSTER CROWING SFX)

Chorus #1: Then the cock crew the second time, and Peter remembered the word that Jesus had said to him.

'Before the cock crows twice, you shall deny Me three times.'

And weighing that with himself, he wept. *(exit)*

(MUSIC OUT)

Chapter 15 (All verses)

*(begin **WTB_Mark15u_mix**)*

Chorus #2: *(DSR)* And before dawn, the high Priests held a Council with the Elders, and the Scribes, and the whole Council, and bound Jesus. And led Him away. And delivered Him to Pilate.
Then Pilate asked him,

(MUSIC OUT)

(during the next exchange, Pilate is on the first riser and Jesus is DSL. Like with the High Priest, they are speaking to each other but both facing the audience)

Pilate: Are You the King of the Jews?

Jesus: It is as you say.

(SFX - CROWD COMMOTION)

Chorus #2: And the high Priests accused Him of many things. So Pilate asked Him again,

Pilate: Answer You nothing? Behold how many things they witness against You.

Chorus #2: But Jesus answered no more at all, so that Pilate marveled.

(OMINOUS MUSIC UP AND UNDER)

Chorus #2: Now at the feast, Pilate would deliver a prisoner to them, whomever they would desire. And there was one named Barabbas, bound with his fellows, who had made insurrection, during which he had committed murder.

(VOCAL CROWD SFX UP AND UNDER)

Chorus #2: And the people cried aloud, and began to desire that Pilate would do as he had always done for them.

Pilate: *(with hands raised, to audience, as CROWD NOISE DIMINISHES)*

Should I let loose to you the King of the Jews!?

(CROWD SFX: "GIVE US BARABBAS! WE WANT BARABBAS!")

Chorus #2: For Pilate knew that the high Priests had delivered Him out of envy. But the high Priests had moved the people to desire Barabbas.

(CROWD NOISE DIMINISHES AGAIN as Pilate raises hands.
Note: this next little section needs to be timed out precisely with the soundtrack to work properly. It should really sound and look like Pilate is conversing with the recording--i.e. the crowd)

Pilate: But!....What would you have me do with Him whom you call the King of the Jews?!

(CROWD SFX: "CRUCIFY HIM!")

Pilate: But!

(CROWD DIES DOWN ONE LAST TIME...SHHH! SHHH!!)

What evil has He done!?

(CROWD SFX: "HE IS A TRAITOR TO ROME AND TO GOD! CRUCIFY HIM!!" The volume and vehemence of these last few exclamations by the crowd give Pilate more than a bit of pause at the possibility of antagonizing them any further, and we need to see that in his face.
THE COMMOTION BUILDS A BIT MORE...THEN TRAILS UNDERNEATH AS THE MUSIC COMES BACK UP *and 2 soldiers lead Jesus away)*

Chorus #2: *(moves DCS)* So Pilate, willing to content the people, gave them Barabbas, and delivered Jesus, after he had scourged him, that He might be crucified.

(as the three Choruses speak, they all move to center stage, next to each other, looking out over the audience, as if witnessing the crucifixion. These lines are spoken with little emotion, not quickly, but not wasting any time either, like detached news reporters delivering a story.)

(SFX_SOLDIERS MOCKING AND BEATING JESUS)

Chorus #1: *(entering SL and moving DCL, next to Chorus #2)*
Then the soldiers led Him away into the hall, which is the common hall, and called together the whole band. And clad Him with purple. And made a crown of thorns and put it on His head.
And began to salute Him, saying, "Hail, King of the Jews."

Chorus #3: *(entering SR and moving DCR, next to Chorus #2)*
And they struck Him on the head with a staff. And spit on Him, and bowed their knees, and did Him reverence.

Chorus #2: And when they had mocked Him, they took the purple off Him, and put His own clothes on Him, and led Him out to crucify Him.

(SFX – 'VIA DOLOROSA' CROWD MOCKING)

Chorus #1: And they compelled one that passed by called Simon of Cyrene who came out of the country, and was father of Alexander and Rufus, to bear His cross.

(SFX – NAILING)

Chorus #2: And they brought Him to a place named Golgotha. Which is by interpretation, "The place of dead mens' skulls". And they gave Him wine to drink, mingled with myrrh. But he refused it.

Chorus #3: And when they had crucified Him, they parted His garments, casting lots for them, what every man should have.

(all three Choruses follow the Cross upward with their eyes, tears forming as they speak)

Chorus #1: And it was the third hour when they crucified Him.

Chorus #2: And the title of His cause was written above.

All in Unison: THAT KING OF THE JEWS.

(they all continue to look up at the Cross)

Chorus #3: They crucified also with Him two thieves, the one on the right hand, and the other on His left.

Chorus #1: Thus the Scripture was fulfilled, which says, 'And He was counted among the wicked.'

(During these speeches, the Choruses slowly turn toward the Heckler and the High Priest respectively, to acknowledge them.)

Chorus #2: And they that went by railed on Him, wagging their heads,

(SFX – [SR] HEY! YOU WHO WOULD DESTROY THE TEMPLE, AND BUILD IT IN THREE DAYS! SAVE YOURSELF! AND COME DOWN FROM THE CROSS!)

Chorus #3: Likewise also even the high Priests mocking, said among themselves with the Scribes,

(SFX – [SL] HE SAVED OTHER MEN. HIMSELF HE CANNOT SAVE. LET CHRIST, THE KING OF ISRAEL NOW COME DOWN FROM THE CROSS, THAT WE MAY SEE, AND BELIEVE.)

Chorus #1: They also that were crucified with Him, reviled Him.

(GATHERING STORM SFX, THUNDER)

Chorus #2: *(Choruses move DSR in very close ranks now, still looking up at Cross)* Now when the sixth hour was come, darkness arose over all the land until the ninth hour. And at the ninth hour, Jesus cried with a loud voice, saying,

(the rest of Jesus' lines in this chapter are recordings, spoken "from the Cross" offstage. The focus remains on those who must watch the crucifixion from the stage)

Jesus: *(recorded)* Eloi! Eloi! Lama-sabachthani!?

Chorus #3: Which is by interpretation, 'My God! My God! Why have You forsaken Me?' And some of them that stood by, when they heard it, said,

Bystander #1: *(SL)* Behold, he calls Elijah.

Chorus #1: And one ran, and filled a sponge full of vinegar, and put it on a staff, and gave it to Him to drink, saying,

Bystander #2: *(SL, reaching for Jesus with the staff, then finally retreating)* Let Him alone! Let us see if Elijah will come, and take Him down.

*(a long pause precedes **JESUS' AGONIZING FINAL WAIL FROM THE CROSS BEFORE HIS DEATH. ALMOST SIMULTANEOUSLY, VIOLENT CRASHES OF THUNDER AND LIGHTNING BEGIN** as everyone onstage falls to the ground, covering their faces in blinded awe and fear)*

Chorus #2: *(shielding eyes from storm, even kneeling down possibly)* And Jesus cried with a loud voice, and gave up the ghost!

*(**A VERY LARGE, ALMOST ELECTRIC-SOUNDING CRASH IS HEARD RIPPING THROUGH THE SKY AND INTO THE TEMPLE CURTAIN**, with a large flash of light, as everyone is knocked off their feet)*

Chorus #3: *(also caught up in the storm)* And the veil of the Temple was torn in two, from the top to the bottom!

*(**SLOWLY, OVER THE COURSE OF 10-15 SECONDS, THE STORM SFX BEGIN TO SUBSIDE**. Choruses rise to their feet)*

Chorus #1: Now when the Centurion who stood near Jesus, saw that He thus crying gave up the ghost, he said,

Centurion: *(SL, looking up and out toward audience also, at Jesus on the Cross)* Truly this man was the Son of God.

*(**ETHEREAL MUSIC UP AND UNDER**)*

Chorus #1: *(looking out over audience)* There were also women who beheld afar off, among whom was Mary Magdalene, and Mary the mother of James the less, and of Joses, and Salome. Who, when Jesus was in Galilee, followed Him, and ministered to Him. And there were many other women who had come up with Him to Jerusalem.

Chorus #2: *(from first step of risers. During the next three lines, 3 or 4 actors on the risers pick up and carry another actor, or "Jesus' body", offstage through the BOH)*

And now when the night was come (because it was the Day of the Preparation, that is before the Sabbath), Joseph of Arimathea, an honorable counselor, who also looked for the kingdom of God, went in boldly to Pilate and asked for the body of Jesus.

Chorus #3: *(moving DSL)* And Pilate marveled that Jesus was already dead. And he called to him the Centurion and asked of him whether Jesus had been any while dead.

Chorus #1: And when he knew the truth from the Centurion, he gave the body to Joseph, who bought a linen cloth and took Him down and wrapped Him in the linen cloth, and laid Him in a tomb that was hewn out of a rock.

Chorus #2: And he rolled a stone to the door of the sepulcher. And Mary Magdalene, and Mary Joses' mother, beheld where He was laid.

Chapter 16 (All verses)

*(Begin **WTB_Mark16u_mix**)*

Chorus #3: *(DSL as the women enter USL and move DSR)*

And when the Sabbath day was past, Mary Magdalene, Mary the mother of James, and Salome bought sweet ointments, that they might come and anoint Jesus. Therefore early in the morning, the first day of the week, they came to the sepulcher, when the Sun was now risen.

Magdalene: Who shall roll away the stone from the door of the sepulcher?

(MUSIC CHANGE)

Chorus #3: And when they looked, they saw that the stone was rolled away. For it was a very great one. So they went into the sepulcher, and saw a young man sitting at the right side, clothed in a long white robe. And they were quite awestruck. But he said to them,

Angel: *(DSR, to them)* Be not so stricken! You seek Jesus of Nazareth, Who has been crucified. He is risen! He is not here. Behold the place where they put Him. But go your way, and tell His disciples, and Peter, that He will go before you into Galilee. There you shall see Him, as He said to you.

Chorus #3: *(spoken as the two Marys and Salome exit through the audience and out the BOH)*

And they went out quickly and fled from the sepulcher. For they trembled and were amazed. Neither said they anything to any man. For they were afraid.

(Both Angel and Chorus #3 exit. The remaining text is spoken offstage as the lights slowly build to a warm, intense morning glow before fading to black after "Amen.".)

Chorus #2: And when Jesus was risen again, early the first day of the week, He appeared first to Mary Magdalene, out of whom He had cast seven devils. And she went and told them that had been with Him, which mourned and wept. And when they heard that He was alive, and had appeared to her, they believed it not.

Chorus #1: After that, he appeared to two of them in another form, as they walked and went into the country. And they went and told it to the remnant. And they didn't believe them.

Chorus #2: Finally, He appeared to the eleven as they sat together, and reproached them for their unbelief and hardness of heart. And he said to them,

Jesus: Go into all the world, and preach the Gospel to every creature. He that shall believe and be baptized, shall be saved. But he that will not believe, shall be damned. And these signs shall follow them that believe; in my Name they shall cast out demons, and shall speak with new tongues, and shall take away serpents. And if they shall drink any deadly thing, it shall not hurt them. They shall lay their hands on the sick, and they shall recover.

Chorus #3: So after the Lord had spoken to them, he was received into heaven, and sat at the right hand of God. And they went forth, and preached everywhere. And the Lord wrought with them, and confirmed the word with signs that followed. Amen.

(fade to black)

Also available from Steve Cook:

Memo Devo: Memorization as Devotion
Devotionals Designed to Help You
Begin to Activate More Scripture in your Life

What if there was a way to experience more of God's power in my life and be a more effective witness for God, using only the time and resources I already possess? I'd have an inexpensive way to achieve two of my main spiritual goals: better intimacy with God and a better witness for God. Since I started memorizing long passages of Scripture in 2009, I have drawn closer than ever to Jesus and gained new peace and confidence in sharing the Gospel. Memo Devo is designed to help you do the same thing and begin to activate more Scripture in your life so that you can love Jesus better than you ever have before. Just as He promised. (Jn15:7-8,17:17)

*"The children see Jesus through Steve.
The love he has for Him really shines through."*

-Rosalyn Johnston, Discipleship Coordinator, Perimeter Church, Atlanta GA

*"From the moment I met Steve
his incredible giftings were quite evident.
A master of character voices,
his servant's heart shines through in every situation."*

-Frank Montenegro, Voice of Dr. Kendall Park, Creationworks' 'Jonathan Park'

*"Steve is gifted in ways most actors are not.
And to know that he is using his talents
to glorify the Word and the Lord
are inspiring to me."*

-Brad Sherrill, Actor, The Gospel of John

www.5talentsaudio.com

www.ingramcontent.com/pod-product-compliance
Lightning Source LLC
Chambersburg PA
CBHW060426050426
42449CB00009B/2150